Sandyford Road, Dublin 16
Telephone: 01 2078513
Email: knowledge@imi.ie
http://www.imi.ie

Welcome

Welcome to the start of a wonderful journey. When you reach the end of this book you will have discovered a new insight into your actions and behaviours. You will have a new understanding of interpersonal skills and have the ability to positively affect your personal and professional relationships.

DF Leap

1

The Dirty Dozen

Dealing with difficult people

Derek E Fox

DF-Leap

www.DFLeap.com
info@dfleap.com

All images provided by Graham Ogilvie

http://www.ogilviedesign.co.uk/

Content:

I dedicate this book to all the wonderful people who have encouraged me to overcome dyslexia and capture my thoughts and tips in text. Thank you.

Chapter One: Identifying Difficult People

Understanding the motivation behind the behaviours

1

Identifying Difficult People
(and their behaviours)

We can all be difficult from time to time, when we are under pressure or when we are tired and frustrated. Difficult behaviours can be dealt with through knowledge and understanding of the DiSC model of human behaviour.

Difficult people are the ones we cannot stand to be around, their behaviours drive us mad. They never seem to do what you want them to do and they are always causing you stress and difficulty. We cannot understand or accept their behaviour as we think it is not appropriate. We can be frightened of their behaviours if they are forceful and bullying, frustrated if they are stubborn or demanding, annoyed if they are self-centred, or agitated if they are a know it all.

Difficult people come with a range of difficult behaviours. This chapter will look at the 12 most common difficult behaviours found in the workplace. We will explore and define these 'Dirty Dozen' of difficult behaviours, understand where they come from, and identify the intent behind the behaviours.

The Dirty Dozen
(the 12 most difficult behaviours)

The Bully
Pushy and ruthless, loud and forceful, the bully knows what he/she wants and how to get it. If you are in their way or standing against them they will either cut you down or steamroll over you. They are single minded and not afraid to focus in like a laser on a person or issue. There is no discussion with the bully, it is their way or no way.

The Sniper

Operates behind your back taking pot-shots at you or your credibility. They seek out your weaknesses and exploit them. In the workplace they covertly work against you. For some reason they resent you or your position. They don't get mad, they get even.

The Volcano

Like a ticking time-bomb you are just waiting for this person to explode. When they do it is always disproportionate to the situation. Everyone around them tries to head for higher ground and escape the torrent of their venting.

The Expert

The expert knows everything, just ask them, actually you won't have to! They are always telling you and not listening to a word you say since your ideas are not as good as theirs.

The Bluffer

The bluffer tries to show he/she is an expert at everything. No matter what the topic or situation is they will have an input and boast of their experience in this area. They often give the wrong information or advice but never admit responsibility.

The Agreer (Agree-er)

Always saying yes, but often leaving you disappointed the agreer over commits and under delivers. They are always trying to please everyone by agreeing with them, even when agreeing is in contradiction to a previous agreement!

The Avoider

Go on; just try to get the avoider to make a decision. They are the experts in procrastination; every question is answered with a 'maybe'. They never commit and avoid taking action. The avoider believes that if they wait long enough someone else will make the decision or take action.

The Void

You just cannot tell what is going on because the void tells you nothing, no feedback, no verbal hints, no body language, just a blank response. The more you push the less you get. Getting anything out of the void is like drawing blood from a stone.

The Doomsayer

'This won't work, that won't work' and 'no, that's no good' are just some of the doomsayer's favourite sayings. They have the ability to see what is wrong with everything. They are very negative to any new ideas but defend their actions by saying they are just being realistic. The doomsayer is discouraging and sees a cloud on every silver lining.

The Whinger

The world is against this person and they love telling everyone about it. The whinger constantly whines about everything and everyone, they love to wallow in their own woe. No matter what you say to the whinger they will complain about it. The whinger believes it is all everyone else's fault and they are not prepared to do anything about it except whinge.

The Controller

This person wants to do everything and be involved in everything. They love to take control. If you are managing a project and they are on the team, watch them take over and try to control everything. They do this in front of you and behind your back. You arrive into work finding they have changed your plan or schedule without asking.

The Waster

You know this person does nothing but no one seems to do anything about it. While everyone else is busy they swan around talking about how busy they are but never doing anything. When you ask them to help out they have a hundred and one excuses why they cannot help. When their work is late/not done again they have a list of excuses, it is never their fault.

Did you recognise anyone in the list? Maybe you recognised a few people, or the same person with a few of the behaviours. If your work colleagues read the list would they recognise you?

These are the 12 most difficult behaviours in the workplace that people have to deal with on a regular basis. Difficult people are not limited to this 'Dirty Dozen' of behaviours, however, these are the top 12 most common difficult behaviours taken from research in the workplace.

As you know we can all be difficult from time to time when our needs are not being met or when we are frustrated, however, difficult behaviours are more regular and systemic. Difficult people display these behaviours on a regular basis. To deal effectively with these behaviours and get difficult people to be less difficult it is important to understand the intent behind each of the behaviours. As you will see the intent is positive it is just the impact of the behaviours that is difficult. When we understand the intent behind someone's behaviours we can better deal with their behaviours. Instead of just judging them on their behaviour, we have a deeper understanding and can see why they are behaving this way. We may not agree with it, but we can understand it. This helps use to be able to deal more effectively with the difficult behaviour.

The next set of chapters will explore specific strategies for dealing with each of the 12 difficult behaviours, for now we need to explore and understand the intent behind the 12 behaviours. To help you reach a better understanding of the intent behind the behaviours we will relate them to the DISC model of human behaviour and identify the underlying needs and motivation behind each of the DISC behavioural styles.

The DISC Model

Here we will introduce the DISC model and look at the basic understanding of Dominance, Influence, Steadiness and Conscientiousness.

The DISC model identifies your level of each one of the behavioural factors, whether you are a high or low D for dominance, a high or low I for influence, a high or low S for steadiness, or a high or low C for conscientiousness. The DISC model will show you your blended style across all four behaviour factors. Less than 2% of the population are what is known as a pure style, i.e. a person that is high in only one behaviour factor and low in the other three. For the purpose of introduction and to help you understand the DISC model we will focus on initially describing the basic behaviour factors of the DISC model. As your knowledge and understanding develops you can start to look at blended styles across all four behavioural factors, for example what does someone with a high D and high I look like versus someone that has a high D, low I and high S etc.

The Basic Model

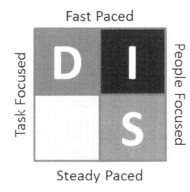

The basic model works across two dimensions. The first dimension looks at your pace, either fast-paced or steady-paced. The second dimension looks at your focus, either task focused or people focused. Depending on your pace and focus this will direct you towards D, I, S or C.

Someone who is both fast-paced and task focused can be described as a high D for dominance. Someone who is fast-paced and people focused can be described as a high I for influence. Someone who is steady paced and task focused can be described as a high C for conscientiousness. Someone who is steady paced and people focused can be described as a high S for steadiness.

Very quickly you can take a look at someone's behaviours and diagnose their pace and focus to identify which behavioural style best describes their behaviour whether it be D I S or C.

D —Dominance

We can describe a person who is fast-paced and task focused as a high D for dominance. A high D can be described as:

- *Results orientated*
- *Goal focused*
- *Action orientated*
- *Decisive and direct*

A person with a high D factor likes to achieve results, has a desire to take control, and is very competitive. They are very comfortable accepting challenges, they can be strong willed and impatient. They are quick to take action and are very innovative. High D's have a tendency to love power and authority, they also have a preference for direct answers. They may have high egos and drive hard for results. They like challenges and are natural problem solvers. Their strong focus on results may be seen by others as overly aggressive behaviour and some D's may be described as being a bully or being too directive when dealing with others.

I –Influence

We can describe a person who is fast-paced and people focused as a high I for influence. A high I can be described as:

- *People orientated*
- *Optimistic and encouraging*
- *Enthusiastic and open*
- *Expressive and outgoing*

A person with a high I factor likes to receive recognition and praise; they are influential and enthusiastic towards their tasks and goals. They may be described as very entertaining and expressive; they can be very talkative and enjoy dealing with people. High I's can be described as socially and verbally aggressive, they are energising and help motivate others. A high I can be seen as overly dependent on interaction with other people and seem overly needy of recognition and praise.

S –Steadiness

We can describe a person who is steady paced and people focused as a high S for steadiness. A high S can be described as:

- *Stable and cooperative*
- *Good listener, sympathetic*
- *Good team worker, dependable*
- *Diplomatic and consistent*

A person with a high S factor likes to avoid conflict and will always seek harmony. They can be described as very loyal to those they identify with, they are good listeners and very patient with others. They dislike rapid or constant change preferring instead to focus on security and stability.

They like to work within a predictable environment, preferring to work in an environment where traditional and steady procedures are adopted. They have an orientation towards family activities and values. They may procrastinate over decision-making and will avoid giving constructive feedback.

C – Conscientiousness

We can describe a person who is steady paced and task focused as a high C for conscientiousness. A high C can be described as:

- *Analytical and accurate*
- *Orderly and disciplined*
- *Quality conscious*
- *Deliberate and systematic*

A person with a high C factor likes to reflect on situations before taking action. They want to analyse the facts and figures or pros and cons of the situation before making a decision. They are objective thinkers with a tendency to be perfectionists. They set high standards and are well disciplined in delivering accurate results in line with expectations, processes, and/or procedures. They are motivated by the right way to proceed, and will always seek justice in a given situation. The high C's may be seen as cold and withdrawn by others.

These four basic factors of D, I, S, and C make up the DISC behavioural model. Each of the factors has their own unique traits and strengths that will define their individual behavioural style.

Exploring the intent /motivation behind the DISC behaviours:

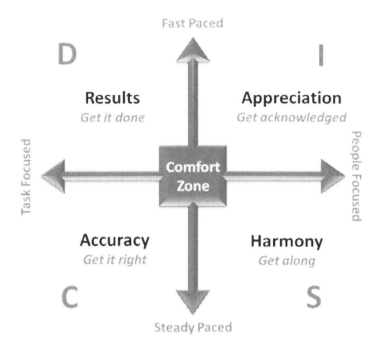

Understanding the four intents:

- **D** – *Dominance – Results, get it done*
- **I** – *Influence – Appreciation, get acknowledged*
- **S** – *Steadiness – Harmony, get along*
- **C** – *Conscientiousness- Accuracy, get it right*

Results:
The D-style behaviours are a result of the underlying need and motivation to get it done and achieve a result. The positive side of this motivation is the focus on results, the innovation and drive for achievement and the ability to overcome difficult

situations and/or issues. The negative side of this motivation is the pushy and dominant behaviours that are displayed when the D-style is not achieving their goal of results, getting it done.

Appreciation:

The I-style behaviours are a result of the underlying need and motivation to get acknowledged and receive appreciation. The positive side of this motivation is the focus on enthusiasm, collaboration, innovation, engagement and action. The negative side of this motivation is the attention seeking, the sulking, the sniping, and the self-centred behaviours that are displayed when the I-style is not achieving their goal of appreciation, getting acknowledged.

Harmony:

The S-style behaviours are a result of the underlying need and motivation to get along and achieve harmony. The positive side of this motivation is the focus on team work, listening, collaboration, and support. The negative side of this motivation is the withdrawn, passive, approval seeking and submissive behaviours that are displayed when the S-style is not achieving their goal of harmony, getting along.

Accuracy:

The C-style behaviours are a result of the underlying need and motivation to get it right and achieve accuracy. It is also important to understand that 'getting it right' also includes justice, or at least the C's perception of justice. The positive side of this motivation is the focus on accuracy, stability, challenge, quality, and analysis. The negative side of this motivation is the picky, perfectionist, negative, and stubborn behaviours that are displayed when the C-style is not achieving their goal of accuracy, getting it right.

Intents continuously change, depending on the person and the situation, which brings changes in behaviour. It helps to:

1. **_Understand the four intents:_**
   They all have their time and place in our lives.

2. **Be attentive to communications:**
   Be aware of words, tone, and body language, they can indicate primary intent.

3. **_Don't be difficult:_**
   When your intents are not met, you may become a difficult person yourself.

When each of the DISC styles are achieving their underlying needs they are in the comfort zone and have the flexibility to interact effectively with all other styles. Once our basic needs are being met we are more tolerable of the people and situations around us.

It is only when the underlying needs are not being met that we start to see the difficult behaviours emerging. Remember that when we are under stress or not achieving our needs we revert to type, or return to norm, meaning we become MORE of our primary DISC style. The D becomes more of a D, the I more of an I, the S more of an S, and the C more of a C. When the underlying needs are not being met people move away from the comfort zone and become less flexible in their approach and behaviours.

Relating the behaviours to the Intents:

Below you will find a basic model relating each of the 12 difficult behaviours to the corresponding intent. It is important to understand that we can display any of the behaviours in a specific situation; the list below shows the most common relationship between the intent and the behaviours.

The Intent	The associated behaviours
Results – Get it Done	The Bully
	The Expert
	The Sniper
	The Controller

The Intent	The associated behaviours
Appreciation – Get acknowledged	The Sniper
	The Volcano
	The Bluffer
	The Waster

The Intent	The associated behaviours
Harmony – Get along	The Volcano
	The Agreer
	The Avoider
	The Void

The Intent	The associated behaviours
Accuracy – Get it right	The Expert
	The Void
	The Doomsayer
	The Whinger

Understanding the behaviours under pressure:

If people are out of their comfort zone for too long they will exaggerate their behavioural style. This is a warning sign, when you observe these behaviours it is time to address them directly and try to help the person achieve their underlying needs. Here are the exaggerated behaviours:

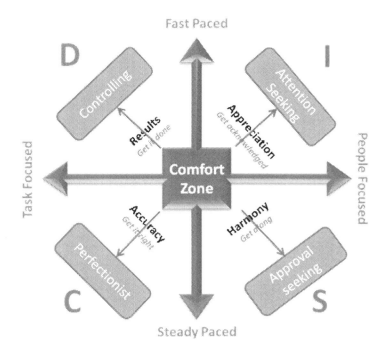

- **D** – *Dominance – becomes controlling*
- **I** – *Influence – becomes attention seeking*
- **S** – *Steadiness – becomes approval seeking*
- **C** – *Conscientiousness- becomes a perfectionist*

Controlling:

The D-style becomes more controlling, they micro-manage everyone and everything. They want all of the details and they want them now. If you cannot give them what they want they will get it themselves. Usually happy with just the bullet points the D-style looks for more and more detail as they become more controlling.

Attention seeking:

Starved of appreciation the I-style will jump and shout until they get attention. This is a cry for help, they are simply stating *'look at me, acknowledge me...'* this may be in the form of over exaggerated behaviours or out of context responses and actions. They may jump in with a smart or snide comment just to get noticed. They can also explode and rant about a situation.

Approval seeking:

Remember the last thing the S-style wants to do is cause conflict, so when they are out of their comfort zone too long they start to seek approval for everything. They do not want to do anything without external approval first just in case it may add to the disharmony.

Perfection seeking:

The C-style will become overly negative and criticise everyone and everything as it falls way below their inflexible standards. They will not be happy until everything is 100%, 99.9% will not do. They become overbearing with the finite details and set unrealistic standards of expectation. Meanwhile they constantly complain that no one cares.

It is important to remember that we can all be difficult from time to time, but when these difficult behaviours become the norm then we become difficult people.

Keep an eye out for the behaviours of the 'Dirty Dozen':

In the next set of chapters we will explore a range of strategies designed to bring out the best in these difficult behaviours.

Chapter two: Bringing out the best in people

Strategies for dealing with difficult people

2

Bringing out the best in people

When it comes to getting the best out of difficult people it is about addressing the behaviour, not the person. We can all have difficult behaviours from time to time, however, when they become the normal behaviour it is time to change your approach and use a new model for success.

Difficult behaviours can cause stress, frustration, and dismay for the people who have to deal with them. If you are on the receiving end of a difficult behaviour you know how it can make you feel. These chapters will introduce you to a range of proven strategies that are designed to bring the best out of people when they are stuck in their difficult behaviour. From changing your mindset and approach to communicating and tactics these strategies will help you deal with difficult people.

Choosing your approach:

1. Understand that everybody reacts differently to these types of behaviour.

The person who's most irritating to you may be perfectly acceptable to someone else.

2. Get to know these people.

Each warrants a different response. Think about the people you know. Does anybody at work or at home display these behaviours?

3. Recognise when you are difficult.

We can all be difficult at times. Understanding these behaviours in yourself will help you understand them in others.

You do have a choice about how you deal with difficult people, actually you have a range of choices, they are:

- *Just put up with it -stay and do nothing*
- *Walk away -vote with your feet*
- *View them differently -change your attitude*
- *Treat them differently -change your behaviour*

Avoid doing nothing. Only walk away when it is the best option. Work on changing your attitude and then your behaviour. You will be amazed at the results.

Even if the difficult person continues to engage in the difficult behaviour, you can learn to see them differently, listen to them differently, and feel differently about them.

A 5-Step approach:

When you need to deal with difficult people and their behaviours here is a simple 5-step approach to increasing your effectiveness:

1. Reduce barriers and differences
2. Listen closely to understand
3. Explore and understand
4. Communicate clearly
5. Focus on the positive and improvement

Reduce barriers and differences

Remember that no one cooperates with anyone who seems to be against him or her.

- Blend your voice and body language to match the other person.
- Blend before you redirect. Only after building rapport can you redirect.
- Match the level of their energy and reflect the emotions they are expressing.
- Use the same language and sayings.
- Talk about 'US' not you and them, remove barriers and differences.

Conflict occurs when the emphasis is on differences. Reducing differences can turn conflict into cooperation.

Listen closely to understand

It is twice as hard to listen than it is to speak, listen hard and listen well. Only when someone feels they are being listening to will they open up and communicate.

- Learn and practice active listening.
- Listen- Show you are listening – ask clarifying questions, summarise, and confirm.
- Make sure the other person knows you have heard and understood.

When two or more people want to be heard and no one is willing to listen, an argument is inevitable. Listen and understand first, and you unlock the doors to understanding and collaboration.

Explore and understand

Seek clarity and understanding of the intent behind the words or behaviours. Try to explore the 'why'. Put yourself in their shoes and see it from their point of view.

- Identify and act on the intent.
- Use criteria to reach deeper understanding. What are the filters (yours and theirs), how can you by-pass these.

This is about the kind of understanding that will help you communicate effectively. Understanding from their point of view will help you create solutions that match.

Communicate clearly

Use simple words and phrases, state the facts, give examples, and check for clarity.

- Monitor your tone of voice, tactfully interrupt, and tell your truth.
- Remember that the word 'communicate' has the same origins as' common' –to communicate is to build a common understanding.

What you say to people can produce defensiveness or trust, increase resistance or cooperation, promote conflict or understanding. Make sure you are focusing on the responses you want to invoke.

Focus on the positive and improvement

Understand and embrace **Pygmalion power**, when you tell someone that they are doing something wrong, they are very likely to get defensive, when you focus on the positive and the required improvement it promotes a positive response.

- Appreciate criticism; this is nothing more than the flip of Pygmalion power.
- It's a fact that people rise or fall to the level of your expectations and projections.

Project and expect the best, remember we see the behaviours we are looking for. Start to look for the positive behaviours, you may just surprise yourself.

Chapter three: Dealing with the Bully

3

Bringing the best out of the Bully

The strategies and models suggested in this chapter are designed to bring the best out of a person that displays this behaviour pattern. Remember we can all be difficult from time to time, these strategies are for dealing with a person who consistently displays this behaviour type.

The Intent

Remember the intent behind the behaviour of the bully is to get it done, they are focusing on results. They need it done now and if you are in the way they will push you aside or push straight through you to get the result.

From their point of view:

The bully is on a mission to get it done, they are unable to slow down or change behaviours as they do not see anything wrong with what they are doing. If you are in the way you need to be removed. They have no problem with pulling you apart personally, however, it is not personal, you just happen to be in the way of them achieving their result.

How to deal with 'The Bully':

If you are under attack from the bully they probably see you as part of the problem. Their aggressive behaviour is to get you doing what they want or get you out of the way and let them do it themselves. Here is what you need to do:

1. Don't back down
2. Take control, interrupt them
3. Address the main issue
4. Focus on results
5. Agree actions

Don't back down:

If you fold like a deckchair the bully will see this as a win and learn that to deal with you all they have to do is push harder.

We give people permission to treat us the way they do through our behaviours and responses. If the bully learns that you agree or get out of the way when they push harder or shout louder then they are going to do this when you are in the way! Stand your ground, you do not need to counter-attack, just stay with your position. Let the bully rant and rave and when they are finished look them in the eye, state your position and move to the next step.

Take control, interrupt them:

If the bully is not giving up and they start all over again when you state your position then you need to take control and interrupt them. A very effective way of doing this is by repeating their names over and over until you have their attention. Stay very assertive (aggressive people actually respect assertive people), keep your voice to about ¾ of the level they are speaking at. Now that you have their attention it is time to move to the next step.

Address the main issue:

Backtrack to the main issue the bully has and address it directly, this shows you were listening and are interested in their concerns. Explain how you understand the situation and ask them to clarify the situation. If they start to rant and rave again go back to the previous step. When they start to explain their perception of the issue make sure you do not judge their opinion, you only want to show you are addressing the same issue as the bully. Now it is time to switch the focus to results.

Focus on results:

Turn the conversation towards what you can and will do. If this is not enough for the bully clearly state again what you can and will do. Even in situations where you totally disagree with the bully tell them exactly what you are going to do. This may simply be ' *I am not going to do that'*, *'here is what I am going to do'*. Keep your language focused towards results, for example, if they are asking you to do something that requires additional resources instead of saying *'I can't do that because...' say 'to do that I will need...'.*

Agree actions

Finally agree actions, who will do what and by when. Make sure it is clear who is responsible for the actions. In situations where you have stated you are not going to do what they want, use this step to agree what they need to do next, and how they need to behave with you going forward, for example, ' *we can't agree on this, you need to find another way to achieve this and when you are ready to discuss this normally I will be here to help you achieve the result'*.

Actions to avoid:

- Never counter-attack the bully.
- Don't defend, explain, or justify your position, just state it assertively.
- Don't shut down, you may be tempted to withdraw but this will send a clear message of victory to the bully and reinforce their difficult behaviour.

The Dirty Dozen

Chapter four: Dealing with the Sniper

4

Bringing the best out of the Sniper

The strategies and models suggested in this chapter are designed to bring the best out of a person that displays this behaviour pattern. Remember we can all be difficult from time to time, these strategies are for dealing with a person who consistently displays this behaviour type.

The Intent

Remember the intent behind the behaviour of the sniper is to get results or to get acknowledged. When the intent is to get results they are using the behaviour of a sniper to control your actions, when the intent is to get acknowledged they are using the behaviour to pull you down and replace you as the centre of attention.

From their point of view:

The sniper has a grudge against you, either they cannot approach you directly or they feel they have to discredit you first. You have what they want and you do not deserve it. Either you hold the key to their goal or you are stealing their limelight. Either way they will try to take you down through covert operations working behind your back to help others see you the same way they do.

How to deal with 'The Sniper':

If you wronged a sniper in some way here is what you need to do:

1. Draw attention to them
2. Ask questions
3. Be assertive, (*use bully strategy if required*)
4. Find out why
5. Agree the future
6.

Draw attention to them:

Your goal is to bring the sniper out of hiding and shine a light on them. Draw attention to their behaviour, even if this is in the middle of a meeting, stop what you are doing, look at them

and repeat the comment they said. Remember the sniper likes to take 'pot-shots' at you, especially when you appear vulnerable. If you overhear the sniper saying '*that is a stupid idea*', stop, look at them and ask '*why do you think this is a stupid idea*'. Once you engage with them it is time to ask questions. If the sniper is deep under cover and you are only hearing the snipes from distance (never catching them in the act), then make it known you are aware of their behaviours. At meetings state you are aware that someone (keep it focused on the individual not a group, never say I am aware that some people are saying...) is saying this or that...

Ask questions:

When you confront the sniper start to ask very assertive and direct questions such as, *'why do you think that?'* or *'what is really behind you comments here?'*. Keep your tone neutral and adopt an inquisitive stance, show that you really do want to know why they feel/think this way.

Be assertive:

Face the sniper head on, if they revert to typical bully behaviours (becoming aggressive, raising their voice, dismissing your questions etc.) then switch to the strategy for dealing with the bully. If they start to complain or get defensive don't let them off with a warning, stay assertive until you identify what the real issue is. You do not need to attack them, just stay assertive, the added attention will draw out their true intention and help you understand if you are dealing with someone who resents you or someone who feels you are in their way for some reason.

Find out why:

Keep using questions to uncover the real issue behind their behaviour. If you do not uncover the issue or address it they will just go on sniping at you afterwards. If they will not answer you directly or are deep under cover then ask open questions to the other people. The goal is to find out why and to understand it. Do not judge their opinion or defend your position, simply try to understand why they feel this way.

Agree the future:

Finally, agree with the sniper what you can and will do. Address their concerns and explain what you expect from them in the future. Make it clear you will not tolerate sniper behaviour and encourage them to come to you directly next time.

Be aware of the 'friendly sniper':

There is another type of sniper; the 'friendly' sniper. Very common in cultures such as Ireland where 'slagging' and sarcasm are part of normal humour. If you become the target of a friendly sniper then simply ignore the comment, laugh with it, or if you feel it is not appropriate then snipe back with good humour, turn the comment back on them in a fun way. For example if they say ' *that's another one of them stupid ideas that management are always coming up with...*' then respond quickly with a witty comment such as ' *well we have to work hard in management to keep up with the crazy ideas you come out with.. How are we doing by the way?*'

The Dirty Dozen

Chapter five: Dealing with the Volcano

5

Bringing the best out of the Volcano

The strategies and models suggested in this chapter are designed to bring the best out of a person that displays this behaviour pattern. Remember we can all be difficult from time to time, these strategies are for dealing with a person who consistently displays this behaviour type.

The Intent

The volcano's behaviour can be driven by their need to get attention and be acknowledged or their need for harmony. Either way they have had enough and their emotions have taken over.

From their point of view:

Enough is enough, they have tried everything they could think of to change the situation but nothing has worked. No one seems to care about the situation or them. How can people allow this to go on this way, it is just not fair. They have had enough; there is no way they can put up with the current situation any longer. This is truly the *'straw that broke the camel's back'*...

How to deal with 'The Volcano':

When they explode they explode on a major scale, this is no simple gripe or whim, they have lost control of rational thinking and they are driven by their emotions, here is what you need to do:

1. Get their attention
2. Show you care
3. Bring them down
4. Let them cool off
5. Don't stoke the fire

Get their attention:

Stand in front of them, call their name, put a gentle hand on their upper arm (be aware of people's personal space needs).

Do whatever you need to get their attention without coming across as aggressive. Make sure your tone of voice is not angry or demanding, you need to come across as concerned and in control. Repeat their name over and over if you need to. If they have stormed off while erupting then you need to make a decision to either go after them if you feel it is right to, or to leave them to cool off and discuss it with them at a later point.

Show you care:

Remember they are highly emotional right now and not typically open to logic or reasoning. The first thing you need to do once you have their attention is show them you care about how they are feeling. Match their intensity but not the emotion. Tell them you can see they are very upset and you want to help, ask them to explain what has happened and help you understand how they are feeling. Listen closely and provide reassurance as they speak. Never judge their reasons just listen and understand.

Bring them down:

As you notice them calming down, start to lower your voice and try to reduce the intensity, allow them to talk it out. Just by listening you are helping them to become calm. Never judge them or start to tell them what they should be doing, just listen and reassure them. The time for addressing the issue and/or behaviour comes later; your focus now is to get them back in control of their emotions. Keep your tone encouraging and make sure you are using non aggressive body language (avoid pointing or making negative facial gestures).

Let them cool off:

If their adrenaline is still pumping and you feel the time is not right to discuss alternative behaviour or to address the issue without them exploding all over again then give them some time to cool off. Let them know you are doing this by saying *'I can see how passionate you are about this right now, why don't you take some time to gather your thoughts and we can discuss this later, say about 3pm, we can grab a coffee or I can drop down to your desk...'* if they are already cool enough and you feel addressing the issue will not set them off again then calmly discuss the issue and or situation with them.

Don't stoke the fire:

Try to identify what sets this person off, why do they explode and where possible avoid setting them off or 'stoking the fire' by bringing up situations and/or issues you know will cause them to erupt. You do not need to 'walk on egg shells' if the situation or issue that sets them off is a normal work situation that is part of the day to day life of their role then additional training/coaching or communication around this is required.

Actions to avoid:

- Don't get aggressive with the volcano, even when you think their behaviour is selfish.
- Avoid judging them on this interaction alone, remember this may be a build up of many things, and make sure you get to know them and what they value.
- Don't isolate them or treat them differently to others, help them integrate and adapt.

The Dirty Dozen

Chapter six: Dealing with the Expert

6

Bringing the best out of the Expert

The strategies and models suggested in this chapter are designed to bring the best out of a person that displays this behaviour pattern. Remember we can all be difficult from time to time, these strategies are for dealing with a person who consistently displays this behaviour type.

The Intent

The behaviour of the expert is driven by the need to get the right result; they are the expert and know exactly what needs to be done. They will either dismiss your inferior ideas or tell you at length why they are inferior. This particular behaviour commonly shares the intent of get it done (results) and get it right (accuracy).

From their point of view:

The expert knows they are the expert, they are number one and everyone else is a distant second. They get frustrated by other people not doing the job to the expert standards they are used to. Why can't everyone else just do it the way they do, it is the best way after all. They have to waste time showing or telling everyone exactly how it is done.

How to deal with 'The Expert':

The expert has a proven track record of being right 99.9% of the time, like it or not, you have to respect their expertise and knowledge in their field. The easiest way to bring the best out the expert is by the following strategy:

1. Do your research
2. Acknowledge their expertise
3. Share their concerns
4. Suggest ideas indirectly
5. Use their strengths

Do your research:

Make sure you have your facts and information correct before you approach the expert, do your homework/research first.

If you are unsure of a topic or what you need to address the expert will rip through the flaws in your idea. Make sure you have a logical approach that deals with facts and figures, avoid bringing in emotions or personal opinions. The expert enjoys a good debate when the focus is on facts and logic. The expert will try to make you feel inferior so earn their respect by showing you have prepared well for this interaction and that you are knowledgeable in this area.

Acknowledge their expertise:

Let them know you respect their knowledge and expertise. Reassure them that they are the expert in this area and that you want to discuss an idea with them to improve efficiency or effectiveness. You are looking for their input to the idea to perfect it. Allow them to give you their ideas, where they are dismissive of your idea, ask them what they would do to achieve the desired outcome. If you want them to listen to your idea and not dismiss it straight off you need to make sure the expert sees how their input is required in this area.

Share their concerns:

If the expert is complaining about the current situation and/or idea, share their concerns, explore why they are concerned about the situation and/or idea. Try to identify if their primary intent is to get it done or to get it right. Once you have identified their primary intent and their main concerns you can blend your language and approach to address these areas directly. Explain how your idea will achieve the result or accuracy they desire, and also reduce or remove their concerns.

Suggest ideas indirectly:

Now it is time to redirect the expert to your idea, however, you need to do this indirectly. Saying straight out *'here is what I think you should do...'* will only send the expert back to step 1 where they see your idea as inferior. Use language such as *'maybe', 'perhaps', 'what would happen if'* and *'we'* instead of *'I'*. Avoid challenging them directly, try to introduce your ideas as alternatives to achieving the same goals.

Use their strengths:

One of the things the expert enjoys is showing/telling others how to do it right. Encourage them to do this now with the new idea. Turn them into a mentor by asking them to make sure everyone is up to speed and proficient on this new task or process. Get them focused on showing/telling others about the idea. Also from time to time go to them for advice, let them know you respect their knowledge. Over time they will begin to see you as a peer and not someone who is inferior to them.

Actions to avoid:

- Resist being a 'know it all' yourself when engaging with an expert this will just focus them on proving you wrong.
- Don't resent the expert; they are a valuable asset to everyone when focused in the right direction.
- Never try to force your ideas on to the expert, take your time, be flexible and patient.

The Dirty Dozen

Chapter seven: Dealing with the Bluffer

7

Bringing the best out of the Bluffer

The strategies and models suggested in this chapter are designed to bring the best out of a person that displays this behaviour pattern. Remember we can all be difficult from time to time, these strategies are for dealing with a person who consistently displays this behaviour type.

The Intent

The bluffer is looking for attention and appreciation. They are driven by the need to be acknowledged. There is nothing more the bluffer loves than to be told *'we couldn't have done this without you!'*.

From their point of view:

The bluffer really wants to help out, they love being the centre of attention and having everything revolve around them. They want to help out everywhere even if the area is not their field of expertise. From time to time they get in over their heads in a situation but they do not want to lose face or have you think they cannot help so they try to bluff their way out of it. It's easier to come up with an excuse than admit they are wrong or do not know.

How to deal with 'The Bluffer':

The bluffer can cause untold damage to tasks and teams by leading people in the wrong direction, they can also build a reputation where people automatically dismiss their input due to past experiences, to get the best out of the bluffer try this:

1. Acknowledge them
2. Get specific
3. Take control
4. Let them off
5. Acknowledge what they can do

Acknowledge them:

Acknowledge their intent and enthusiasm; let them know you appreciate their help and involvement. This will relax them.

You want to create a friendly environment for the bluffer, remember one of their biggest fears is losing face or thinking people are against them. Try to acknowledge any recent successes they have had or contributed towards. Once they are comfortable turn your attention to the issue at hand.

Get specific:

Ask them to explain the current situation, what happened and what they think about it. Try to get them to be specific, the bluffer will tend to generalise and blame other people, however, you need to redirect them back to the specifics and their input and/or responsibilities. If the information they are giving you is misleading or wrong direct them back to what is correct and explore the areas they are wrong about. Give them suggestions and hints towards the correct answers and try to allow them to discover the right answers themselves. If they are unable to do this and maintain their position then it is time to take control and explain the right course of action.

Take control:

If the bluffer is not taking the hint and they continue to bluff then it is time to step in and take control. Interrupt the bluffer politely and tell them the right course of action or the correct answer. You do not need to 'rub it in their face', simply state *'here is what I think you should do...'* explain why you think this is the right course of action and get them to acknowledge it. If needed you can position it as *'if you did this... that would be great and the team would be really thankful to you'*. Make sure they know and understand what you have asked them to do, and get them to tell you how they will do it.

Let them off:

Above all, don't make the bluffer feel you are calling their bluff in an aggressive way. There is no need to back them into a corner and have them admit they are wrong, this is not going to help the situation, it may make you feel good, but remember you want to get the best out the bluffer so focus them on the correct course of action and let them off. It may help to focus on their positive intent, after all they are only trying to help.

Acknowledge what they can do:

Bluffers quickly build up a reputation of being a 'think they know it all' and people start to avoid them and/or dismiss their input without considering it. This is a dangerous cycle for two reasons, 1- you may dismiss a good idea, and 2- the lack of appreciation will only cause them to seek out more attention and increase these difficult behaviours. Try to acknowledge what they are good at, focus on their achievements and encourage their enthusiasm.

Actions to avoid:

- Try to avoid 'bursting their bubble' if you challenge them directly they will only bluff more or make excuses.
- Never judge them too quickly, a bluffer is not always a bluffer, they can be experts in some areas, listen to their input first and reflect before making a snap judgement.

The Dirty Dozen

Chapter eight: Dealing with the Agreer

8

Bringing the best out of the Agreer

The strategies and models suggested in this chapter are designed to bring the best out of a person that displays this behaviour pattern. Remember we can all be difficult from time to time, these strategies are for dealing with a person who consistently displays this behaviour type.

The Intent

The last thing the agreer wants to do is upset anyone so they tend to say yes to every request. This behaviour is driven by the intent to get along and create harmony. They want to please you and this causes them to make promises they can not keep.

From their point of view:

The agreer really wants to help everyone, they are already snowed under themselves, but since they do not want to push back or upset anyone else they continually say yes to every request. As they are trying to do everything for everyone they typically end up finishing nothing for anybody.

How to deal with 'The Agreer':

The agreer can cause a critical project or task to be delayed, they are unable to meet deadlines due to the amount of work they are trying to undertake, however, when you approach them about it they reassure you it will be done, but it rarely is. Here is what you need to do:

1. Create a safe zone
2. Look for honesty
3. Help them focus
4. Agree small steps
5. Build the relationship

Create a safe zone:

Since the agreer wants harmony above all else you need to create a safe environment for them to discuss issues and challenges. They want to avoid causing problems or issues.

Because of this they will be uncomfortable opening up and discussing what they can and cannot do. Make sure your tone is suitable and your non-verbal communication is welcoming. Let them know it is safe to say 'no' and to push back on requests. Ask them to review what they are currently working on and realistically what they can deliver, and more importantly what they cannot deliver.

Look for honesty:

The agreer will have 101 reasons why they cannot deliver. Avoid the temptation to start giving them solutions to each problem, instead talk honestly and openly to the agreer about their ability to deliver on their commitments. Ask them to explore why they are saying yes to everything and help them to identify a process for planning. If the agreer becomes upset or angry, let them talk it out and move back to step 1 and focus on creating a safe communication environment.

Help them focus:

The agreer needs to develop skills in planning and prioritisation. Help them through this process, give them examples of planning tools and walk them through the steps required. Discuss different prioritisation tools and see which one suits the agreer best. Ask them to work through a few examples based on their current workload and commitments. Encourage them to use a daily to-do list with prioritisation, this will also allow them to push back on requests and focus on following through with their existing commitments. Have them practice saying no by applying the prioritisation tool to a set of typical requests.

Agree small steps:

The next step is to gain commitment from the agreer on how they are going to change their behaviours. Remember it will be difficult for them to change completely over night so agree small steps where they can build up the competence over a period of time. Start with the simple steps to give them confidence and reassurance. Agree to meet on a weekly basis to review how they are doing.

Build the relationship:

The agreer responds best to people and relationships, use every opportunity to build the relationship you currently have with them. Acknowledge their commitment and celebrate their achievements (no matter how small), make sure they understand how this new approach is helping everyone overall.

Actions to avoid:

- Avoid directly blaming the agreer as this will only make them feel ashamed and cause them to revert back to the difficult behaviour to try and please you.
- Never be impatient, remember it takes time to change behaviour.
- Don't remove the help and support too early; the agreer may revert back to previous behaviours. Make sure you stick with it. Give them enough support and help until you notice they are comfortable then start to reduce the support slowly over time.

The Dirty Dozen

Chapter nine: Dealing with the Avoider

9

Bringing the best out of the Avoider

The strategies and models suggested in this chapter are designed to bring the best out of a person that displays this behaviour pattern. Remember we can all be difficult from time to time, these strategies are for dealing with a person who consistently displays this behaviour type.

The Intent

One of the last things the avoider wants to do is upset anyone so they tend to avoid committing to situations where they feel it will cause conflict or problems. This behaviour is driven by the intent to get along and create harmony. They avoid decisions hoping if they wait long enough the decision will make itself or someone else will make it for them.

From their point of view:

The avoider feels stuck in the middle, they can see both sides of an argument and want to agree with both sides to avoid any conflict. They don't want to have to pick and choose between the two sides as this will lead to conflict with the losing side.

How to deal with 'The Avoider':

The avoider sits between procrastination and indecision. They seem to be unable to make a decision especially if it is a critical one. Their typical language is '*maybe*' and '*I'll get back to you*'. When dealing with the avoider here is what you should do:

1. Create a safe zone
2. Find out why
3. Help them make decisions
4. Offer support
5. Build the relationship

Create a safe zone:

Since the avoider wants harmony above all else you need to create a safe environment for them to discuss issues and challenges. They want to avoid causing problems or issues.

Because of this they will be uncomfortable opening up and discussing why they are unable to make a decision. Make sure your tone is suitable and your non-verbal communication is welcoming and non-judgemental. Let them know it is safe to discuss issues and problems, this is not about taking sides, it is about understanding issues and finding solutions. Help them understand that by making a decision they are helping others, and by avoiding the decision they are only frustrating both sides.

Find out why:

It is important to surface any conflicts they currently have or are aware of. Help them understand how focusing on the decision will reduce the conflict, it is about the task not the person. Listen carefully to their concerns, where you hear words like *'I think so'*, *'maybe'* or 'that *could be'* this is a signal to dig deeper and seek clarification, try to understand their view of the situation and what they feel may happen. Once you have explored the reasons as to why they are avoiding the decision it is time to help them make the decision.

Help them make decisions:

Show them a range of decision making processes; find a number of processes that fit their needs. Walk them through the steps of decision making focusing on separating the people from the process (it is not about people, it is about the decision). Have them try out a few processes on a current decision they are avoiding and explore the potential outcomes. Get them to commit to a few decisions now.

Offer support:

Once the decision is made show them how you are going to support the decision, help them understand that there is no perfect decision in all situations. They need to make a decision based on the current information. Offer support in discussing future decisions over the short term (but avoid setting up a routine where they come to you for EVERY decision). Where they are still struggling with decisions it may be helpful to suggest training and/or coaching to develop these skills.

Build the relationship:

The avoider responds best to people and relationships, use every opportunity to build the relationship you currently have with them. Acknowledge their commitment to making a decision and celebrate their achievements (no matter how small), make sure they understand how this new approach is helping everyone overall. Seek them out from time to time to help with your decisions, show them you respect their new ability to make decisions.

Actions to avoid:

- Never push them for a quick decision, allow them to take 'reasonable' time to explore the options first.
- Do not lose your temper, you need to stay calm and focused, help the avoider understand it is not about the people and emotions, it is about the decision and actions.
- Try to resist applying too much pressure for a decision. Use the steps covered to help them reach crucial decisions.

The Dirty Dozen

Chapter ten: Dealing with the Void

10

Bringing the best out of the Void

The strategies and models suggested in this chapter are designed to bring the best out of a person that displays this behaviour pattern. Remember we can all be difficult from time to time, these strategies are for dealing with a person who consistently displays this behaviour type.

The Intent

The void will typically withdraw in difficult situations, however, this behaviour may be driven by the need for harmony or accuracy. When the intent is to get along and create harmony the behaviour is to avoid conflict. When the intent is about justice and getting it right the behaviour is to avoid the wrong outcome, or at least attachment to the wrong outcome.

From their point of view:

The void chooses to withdraw and give little or no input as they are uncomfortable with the current situation, either they feel it is wrong or they are concerned about the impact of the outcome on people. They strongly believe the saying '*if you have nothing nice to say then say nothing at all*'.

How to deal with 'The Void':

It can be like drawing blood from a stone, but you need to get input from the void, there is no quick fix but here is a strategy that will help you achieve your goal:

1. Take your time
2. Explore for information
3. Probe for reasons
4. Guess their thoughts
5. State the impact

Take your time:

Dealing successfully with the void may take a long time. If you are in a rush or working under a time constraint, you may be

too intense to draw him/her out. The more intense you are the more the void will withdraw and offer nothing in response. Plan ahead and pick a time and location that will give you at least an hour of undisrupted time to work through the situation with the void. It may also help to send an email and/or memo in advance fully describing what you would like to talk about and why. The wording of this email/memo is critical, it needs to be open and inviting, the focus should be on discussion and understanding, exploring the situation, you do not want to push for an outcome as this will only cause the void to withdraw further and build up a strong barrier before the meeting.

Explore for information:

Ask open ended questions when engaging with the void. They will try to use as few words as possible so do not make their task easier by asking closed questions. Your focus is on drawing them out and exploring the intent behind their behaviour. You want to find out if their behaviour is about justice (the right/wrong thing to do) or harmony (avoiding conflict with or towards people).

Probe for reasons:

If you are not getting a response from the void then switch to probing for reasons, ask more focused and leading questions to spark a response. Do not over do it with closed, assumptive questions at this stage, you just want to try and probe until you hit a soft spot, look for reaction (as there is usually none) to your statements or questions, this may indicate their intent.

Guess their thoughts:

If all else fails try to guess what their thoughts are, use assumptive statements, put yourself in their shoes and think out the situation and say what you think they may be thinking about it. Talk out loud and rattle of ideas and suggestions. Explore both intents, justice, and harmony, to see if you can get anything from them. Make bold statements and help them understand that if they disagree they need to tell you that or you will take it that they agree with you.

State the impact:

Finally show the void how their continued behaviour of withdrawal is affecting the people around them, start to appeal to the logic and relationship side of your argument. If the intent is more about justice show them how withdrawal is not fair on others, and if the intent is more about harmony, show them how their behaviour is causing frustration and potential conflict.

Actions to avoid:

- Don't jump in; you need to explore the intent first to understand where they are coming from.
- Push too fast, above all else you need to take your time with the void, never push for a quick resolution.
- Avoid losing your temper, stay calm and focused and talk it out with the void.

The Dirty Dozen

Chapter eleven: Dealing with the Doomsayer

11

Bringing the best out of the Doomsayer

The strategies and models suggested in this chapter are designed to bring the best out of a person that displays this behaviour pattern. Remember we can all be difficult from time to time, these strategies are for dealing with a person who consistently displays this behaviour type.

The Intent

The intent behind the doomsayer's behaviour is to get it right. They are focused on accuracy and want it to be 100% correct before they agree. Also they will pull your idea apart and pick out all the issues with it.

From their point of view:

If a job is worth doing it is worth doing right, this is the motto of the doomsayer; however, nothing is ever good enough for them. They can't understand how others cannot see the flaws in what they are suggesting. It is up to the doomsayer to point out the errors and shortcomings of other people's ideas. The doomsayer believes they are doing the right thing and being realistic, there is no point starting something that is not going to work.

How to deal with 'The Doomsayer':

Doomsayers focus on the 20% of an idea that will not work ignoring the 80% that is fine. They bring others down with them and discourage innovation and creativity. If you are faced with a doomsayer here is what you need to do:

1. Agree on negativity
2. Draw on their passion
3. Take your time
4. Beat them to it
5. Use their skills

Agree on negativity:

The worst thing you can do when engaging with a doomsayer is to try and convince them to try and focus on the positives.

This comes later, for now you need to agree with their negativity, allow them to be as negative as they want. Encourage them to tell you everything that is wrong with a situation or idea. Let them talk it out. Do not agree or disagree with their statements (remember you are agreeing with their negativity, not their comments). When they have finally started to slow down and reduce their negativity it is time to engage with their passion.

Draw on their passion:

The doomsayer is focused on accuracy, so engage with that. Once they have 'ranted' enough on what is wrong, start to explore what would be right in their opinion. Ask them what they would do differently and why, focus on the task and not the person. They are passionate about the right result so start to lead the conversation towards what the ideal outcome would be. While focusing on the outcome remind them of current limitations and resources. If they start to be overly negative again then ask them for alternatives.

Take your time:

Take your time when dealing with the doomsayer, they are 'wired' for seeing what will not work, or what is wrong, it will take time for them to acknowledge what is working or what elements are right. Get the doomsayer to explore options where they can work together with others to achieve the right result. Where they cannot agree to this then slowly bring the doomsayer towards a workable compromise, explaining the logic and rational to your suggestion.

Beat them to it:

A good suggestion when dealing with the doomsayer is to 'beat them to the punch' by identifying issues or problems upfront. By suggesting the negatives up front you may get them to respond with a positive statement (so they are picking out what is wrong with your statement), or at least they will agree with you. If you show that you are concerned about the accuracy of the work they will be more flexible in their approach.

Use their skills:

Finally, use the doomsayer for what they are best at, but use them to your advantage. Encourage them to identify problems and issues early in the process and ask them to suggest alternatives. Help others understand that they are attacking the problem not the person. Use language such as ' *thank you for pointing out these problems so we can come up with solutions*', and ' I *know you want this to be right so what can we do...*'. It may also be helpful to slightly adjust your attitude towards the doomsayer by:

Shift your attitude towards:

- Seeing the positive intent in their behaviour, after all they are just overly concerned with getting it right.
- It's not about getting them to stop finding fault with ideas or situations; it's about getting them to be constructive with their criticism.
- Look to acknowledge when they catch something before it has a negative impact on results.

The Dirty Dozen

Chapter twelve: Dealing with the Whinger

12

Bringing the best out of the Whinger

The strategies and models suggested in this chapter are designed to bring the best out of a person that displays this behaviour pattern. Remember we can all be difficult from time to time, these strategies are for dealing with a person who consistently displays this behaviour type.

The Intent

Remember the intent behind the behaviour of the whinger is to get it right, they believe that nothing around here is right and nobody cares about it either.

From their point of view:

The whinger truly believes that the world is against them, nobody cares and they have given up trying to do anything about it. All that is left to do is vent their frustrations on everybody else, after all it is these people that caused the problem in the first place. There is no point in trying to fix anything because there is too much to fix, so what is the point in starting, it won't make a difference overall.

How to deal with 'The Whinger':

Whingers can be very difficult to deal with, they complain about everything and everyone, if you are faced with a whinger here is what you need to do:

1. Let them blow off
2. Grab an issue
3. Ask for solutions
4. Vision of the future
5. Draw a line

Let them blow off:

While the whinger is 'blowing off steam' listen for the main points that they are complaining about. The last thing you may want to do is listen to more whinging but it is a critical step.

Let them complain for 1-2 minutes and try to listen to what they are saying; you will need to identify a specific area to focus on in the next step. It is important to keep your body language and facial gestures neutral while they are complaining, avoid becoming defensive or dismissive. Don't agree or disagree with the whinger, just let them talk.

Grab an issue:

After you have identified a specific area from their complaining grab hold of this area and interrupt them. A good way to interrupt is by saying their name (you may need to repeat this over and over until you get their attention). Once you have their attention ask them to be specific about what is wrong with this area/item. Be careful here, the whinger will want to go back to generic whinges, you need to keep pulling them toward the specific, for example, *'you said the meeting was a waste of time, specifically what part of the meeting was a waste of time?'*. Every time the whinger tries to backtrack to generics repeat the focus question to force them into specifics.

Ask for solutions:

Once you have them talking about a specific issue ask them what they would do to resolve it. Again be careful here as they won't want to look at solutions, they just want to whinge. Keep asking them what they would do to resolve it, what is their suggested solution to the issue. Do not offer any solutions yourself (the whinger will only complain about these!), focus solely on getting the whinger to generate solutions.

Vision of the future:

If they are unable or unwilling to look at solutions then try showing them a vision of the future. Create a perfect vision of the future by asking them a question like *'well in a year's time if everything was fixed what would it look like'*. When they describe what it would be like simply ask them' *ok, so what do we need to start doing now to create this future'*.

Draw a line:

If nothing you do can get the whinger to focus on solutions then it is time to draw the line and walk away. Do not express anger or frustration, simply state (assertively), '*I can't help you until you are willing to focus on solutions, when you want to look at ways we can fix this come and talk to me'*. This is not the ideal outcome but at least they will stop whinging at you. Even in the case of the world's most devoted whinger they will learn through your behaviours that it is pointless whinging at you.

Actions to avoid:

- Never agree or disagree with the whinger, it is about solutions, if you agree or disagree they will increase their level of complaining.
- Avoid offering solutions, the whinger will only start to complain about these also.
- Never confuse whinging with venting, the whinger complains non-stop all of the time. Venting is just letting off steam when things get too much for us.

The Dirty Dozen

Chapter thirteen: Dealing with the Controller

13

Bringing the best out of the Controller

The strategies and models suggested in this chapter are designed to bring the best out of a person that displays this behaviour pattern. Remember we can all be difficult from time to time, these strategies are for dealing with a person who consistently displays this behaviour type.

The Intent

Remember the intent behind the behaviour of the controller is to get it done, they are focusing on results. They want it done now and have no problem stepping in and doing it themselves.

From their point of view:

The task is the most important thing, if other people are not ready to step in and do what is required the controller will. After all it does not matter who does it as long as it gets done. The controller can become impatient and frustrated at other people's lack of urgency towards a task. Sometimes a task needs their focus and urgency as it will never be completed without their control.

How to deal with 'The Controller':

The controller wants to control everything, from planning to delivery they will step in and take charge telling others what to do and how to do it. This behaviour can drive people mad when left unchecked. Here is a good strategy for dealing with the controller:

1. Acknowledge intent
2. Discuss the impact
3. Explore reasons
4. Agree ownership
5. Agree actions

Acknowledge intent:

Behind the difficult behaviour of the controller is a genuine positive intent to get results, they want to get it done now.

Acknowledge this positive intent, let the controller know you admire their commitment to the result. Use language such as *'I can see you are passionate about this'*, or *'I know how important this result is to you'*. Help them understand you are just as concerned and focused on the actual result.

Discuss the impact:

The controller may not be aware of the impact of their behaviour on others (they do not see it as a negative behaviour, after all they are just getting it done). You need to raise their awareness of the impact of their behaviour and how it is limiting the ability of others to achieve results. Use language that they understand to emphasise the impact, show them how their behaviours can cause inefficiency for others. Don't focus on the impact to people, focus on the impact to results, for example *'when you do... that means Joe cannot get...'*.

Explore reasons:

Work with the controller to identify the reasons behind their behaviour, why is it so urgent, why does it have to be done a specific way. Try to address their concerns and keep a focus on the result. Discuss the methods used and the impact on the result. Help them see the bigger picture and how their behaviour is limiting the overall result. If they have a specific issue with a person's ability then ask them *'what does this person need to do to improve'*, encourage them to act as a mentor and enable others to achieve the same level of productivity instead of jumping in and doing it for them.

Agree ownership:

Draw up a list of activities and discuss ownership of items. Make sure the controller clearly knows what they are and are not responsible for. Clearly state the consequences if they step over the agreed line in the future. Agree a process where the controller can raise concerns if they feel something is not getting the level of attention its urgency deserves, instead of them stepping in and taking control.

Agree actions:

Finally agree actions; who will do what and by when. Make sure it is clear who is responsible for the actions. Define a process for checking on progress and adherence. Controllers are very supportive of the quick 'traffic light' report where a RED item needs urgent attention, ORANGE is raising a concern but it is not a 'showstopper', and GREEN is everything is good with this aspect/item.

Actions to avoid:

- Never make it personal with the controller, they are not trying to undermine you, they just want to get it done.
- Don't confuse the controller with a 'political schemer', the schemer is trying to undermine you and get the credit for it (treat these people like a cross between the bully and the sniper).
- Don't ignore the controller's behaviour, sometimes it is easier to ignore them and just do it your way when they are not around, but this only encourages the difficult behaviour.

The Dirty Dozen

Chapter fourteen: Dealing with the Waster

14

Bringing the best out of the Waster

The strategies and models suggested in this chapter are designed to bring the best out of a person that displays this behaviour pattern. Remember we can all be difficult from time to time, these strategies are for dealing with a person who consistently displays this behaviour type.

The Intent

The waster wants everyone to think they are so busy and indispensible; they like to be the centre of attention. This behaviour is driven by the intent to get appreciated, they want acknowledgement (not for what they do, but for who they are).

From their point of view:

The waster actually sees themselves as overworked, they truly believe they are 'up to their eyes' with work, however, they need to let everyone else know this, '*as in this place other people are always trying to offload their work on you*'. Unless you can show just how busy you are you will end up with twice as much work as before.

How to deal with 'The Waster':

The waster swans around telling everyone how busy they are and how important their work is, however they spend more time talking about work than actually doing it. If you need to deal with a waster here is a good strategy to tackle their behaviour:

1. Acknowledge commitment
2. Address results
3. Avoid excuses
4. Get commitments
5. Agree follow up

Acknowledge commitment:

Behind it all the waster is looking for appreciation, give it to them. Acknowledge the areas/task they are delivering on.

The issue you want to address is getting them to deliver more, take on more, or to at least stop going on about how much they think they are doing. Make it a habit of identifying what they are doing well. If you acknowledge their good intent this will reduce their need for others to acknowledge it. Make it clear from the initial discussion you want them to focus on doing things differently.

Address results:

Start to focus on output and results by asking them, how they can achieve more by doing it a different or more efficient way. Look for their input on this and be ready for a backlash of how busy they are and how much they are already doing. Again, keep your focus on the results, acknowledge areas in which they are doing well, and use these areas to draw them out and generate ideas how they can get better results elsewhere or on other aspects of their work. For example 'Joe, *you did a great job with the advertising on the Mitchell campaign, how could you get a similar result with the Jones's account?'*

Avoid excuses:

The waster will have 101 excuses as to why they can't deliver or who is holding them up. Resist the temptation to explore these excuses, instead simply ignore them by stating, '*I'm not asking you why you can't deliver, I need to know what you can do to deliver going forward...'* Every time they bring up an excuse ask them what they need to do to overcome this issue or obstacle.

Get commitments:

Turn the conversation towards actual commitments'. Ask the waster to define what they are going to do, how they are going to do it, and when they are going to do it. If they give a time line that you feel is too long, then redirect them by asking '*what would it take for you to do it by...'* Get the waster to document these commitments and use it to follow up with them.

Agree follow up:

Finally agree how and when you will follow up to review their progress. Use the documented commitments they produced as the guideline for the follow up meeting. If they start to make more excuses when you meet for the follow up start over again from step 3 (avoiding excuses). If needed clearly state the consequences to the waster if they continue to fail to deliver on their commitments.

Actions to avoid:

- Don't threaten the waster up front, try to appeal to their good intent before showing them what will happen if they fail to deliver.
- Avoid getting bogged down with all their excuses, they will have an endless supply, simply redirect them back to the actual results required and what they are going to do about it.
- Never agree with their negative opinions of other people, keep the focus on what they will do, not what others are not doing.

The Dirty Dozen

The Dirty Dozen

Made in the USA
Charleston, SC
07 February 2013